Ways to a Love Song
Eliza Ryder

Copyright Information
This is a work of nonfiction. The events and conversations in this book have been set down to the best of the author's ability, although some names and details have been changed to protect the privacy of individuals.

Copyright © 2020 by Eliza M. Ryder

All rights reserved. No part of this book may be reproduced or used in any manner without written permission of the copyright owner except for the use of quotations in a book review. For more information, address: elizamarieryder@gmail.com

First paperback edition August 2020

Book design by Eliza Ryder

ISBN 9 780578 740034 (paperback)

www.alittletasteofhome.net

Table of Content
Introduction: Why I Dream
Blank Page
I Have… Neck – Audre Lorde
Enough
Dream
Here
A Mockingbird's Song
Understanding
Empathy
The Death of Autumn
A Letter to Myself
Hunted
No More Sorries
Chronic Attachment Disorder
Manifestations of 2020/2021
Why I Dream Big
Wifey Material

To My Family
Questions for Mom
The Five Stages of Grief
Dancing with the Prince
Constant Changing
Biting Words
Lost at Sea
Her Gateway
To My Biological Mother
The Gap
To My Little Girl
Backdoor
Faceless Creature
To My Biological Father

Friends?
To My High School Best Friend

Cuts
Support System
My Magic Unicorn
Snapshot
Fireball
The Traveler
T.H.O.T is My Friend
Just Dance Slayer
For the Boys

Validation
Man Enough
Fix You
If You Have Mercy
Cater
A Woman Scorned
Laws and Attraction
Cover Me
To My Nature Boy
My Quiet Strength
St. Louis
What Was Best
With Silence
Safe
Conclusion

Introduction

Love is a song that doesn't quite follow a predetermined melody or script. Each part of the song so intricate and so important that one cannot exist without the other. Love can be found in all of life's creations. It can be seen in the way the sun shines just a little brighter on the darkest of days and through the rain that cleanses us on the days we feel covered in life's grime. Love can be found in the way our dream's give us an escape from reality and how sometimes reality is better than our dreams. Love has many different shapes and forms, bust most seem to truly only want to pursue the romantic love.

The romantic love that leaves butterflies flying around in your stomach, sparks littering up and down your arms and fireworks going off in your head. Romantic love is finding your support system within your soulmate. Being each other's foundation to build on each other and together. The warm embrace that surrounds you and whispers in your ear everything is going to be okay and lifts you up, by never putting you down. Romantic love is not always everlasting. Sometimes the time on the clock runs out. You nitpick at the faults you find within each other, never letting your partner forget they're not perfect. The times you used to wake up together turns into waking up alone, wondering how things got as bad as they did. It becomes wondering how to go about your daily life and not showing the pain festering within. It becomes hurt and sometimes misplaced anger. feelings of abandonment and loneliness. Often times it will paint the ways in which we love others.

Fun family dinners full of laughter and joy turn into separation. You find yourself standing away from the crowd sipping on your drink believing that no one knows you anymore. You wake up next to a stranger every morning. You try to keep everything and everyone hanging on together by a very fragile thread. You lie in bed awake holding your child knowing that they are the only reason you are still there. But sometimes your children aren't enough. You realize it's better to be happy separate than to feel the way you feel together. Even if that means you have to learn how to do everything by yourself.

You turn to your friends for help. Some of the times they surprise you with their helpfulness, but other times they just disappointment. They make you question when things turned from laughing together and inside jokes to barely speaking and generic congratulation messages. And with everything going wrong you start to believe the problem is you.

So, you start to fall out of love with yourself. That girl in the mirror is no longer you. She has your skin and your hair, but that becomes where the similarities end. So, you start the journey of becoming at peace with yourself and finding the person you've somehow lost. The you that disappeared behind the broken relationships, broken homes, and fake friends.

At times it becomes so unbearable you feel it's easier to pretend that it's not happening or that you can't feel anything. Then comes the days you begin to have break throughs. Your smile becomes a little bit brighter. The sparkle returns to your eyes. You become able to look in the mirror and say to yourself with honesty and clarity, "I love you."

Myself

Blank Page

I stare at this blank page unsure of what to write.

Even when I believe I am filled to the brim,

I am as empty as the words on this page.

**I have studied the tight curls on the back of your neck –
Audre Lorde***

That proudly screams I am a black woman
In a society that breaks their back
trying to emulate something that is supposed to come naturally
But does it I question
as the pitchfork cries war while sparring with an undefeated force
in a historic battle of the mane
Or as my fingers become fragile and brittle as they slave away
To afford the necessities of life that comes in a bottle
Labeled all natural
Sulfate Free
Kind of like I am supposed to be
Free
But it has become such a comical concept
Because even when I am free from other races
I am not free from my own
Where natural is life
And relaxers are betrayal
Brought on by Caucasians
Who didn't know our hairs worth
Only what they deem beautiful
But what if it is also what I see as beautiful
Will that tight curl on the back of your neck
So, different from the straight on the back of mine
Deem me unfit
To be a true African American

Dear Mr. I prefer exotic women because black women are angry,

Please do me a favor, kindly shut the fuck up and open a dictionary. We are so sick and tired of you bitching and moaning about all the things you guys hate within yourselves. And since I know you probably won't pick up the dictionary, I did the work for you as usual.

Exotic used as an adjective: originating in or a characteristic of a distant foreign country. These angry black women aka African American women may have been born here and may live here in the U.S., but we did not originate here. African derived from the continent Africa is a distant foreign land in which these "angry black women" were stolen from long ago just as you black men were and put under a boat. The distant foreign land that is shown in the characteristics of our dark chocolate skin and thick asses/ thighs yall like to rap about so much.

Exotic used as a noun: an exotic plant or animal. These angry black women you like to dog so much are the product of mother nature's love, whom she gifted with the ability to take the herbs from the earth and make medicines to cure black men and their children. She gifted the ability to turn herbs into nourishment for black men's bodies.

Exotic used as an adjective: attractive or striking because colorful or out of the ordinary. Angry black women color is so attractive and so striking that many cultures use tanning beds and tanning lotion just to emulate it. They take our curls, braids, and other hairstyles trying to make it their own. They put fillers in their lips and ass just replicate what is naturally ours. Our very essence is so out of the ordinary that it can only be done by others using synthetic means.

Exotic used as an adjective: of a kind not used for ordinary purposes or not ordinarily encountered. The angry black woman is so out of the ordinary that our bodies are used for scientific and medicinal discoveries.

And as for the angry part, we have every right to be. We have watched our sons killed by policemen for playing with b.b. guns in the park and from walking home. We have watched our black men killed over a counterfeit twenty-dollar bill and for selling their mixtapes in front of a convenience store. We have watched our children get pulled out of cars and tased just trying to make it home from college. We have to watch our children die from malnourishment as we raised the children of the others. We have to make do on a paycheck that is only one/fourth of what our white counterparts make. We have to work twice as hard to make sure the future generations make it out of the projects and get an education kept from us. Most of all we are angry because we constantly and consistently use our bodies as shields to protect you from police, from racists who would love to see you dead, and from our own. We are angry because we know we will continue to do so even though you have the audacity to dog us. You say you love the exotic, but really you just love the idea of someone you can control and break down. Because if you truly love what is exotic you would love black women. We are the very definition of exotic.

   Love,
    A Very Exotic Angry Black Woman

Enough

To never be good enough is to be

a tightly squeezed balloon,

a sponge submerged,

to feel your eyebrow being plucked, and

canines ripping through an infant's gums

to be a pencil that is never fully sharpened,

a jar that never quite filled up

a mushroom picked out and discarded,

and shoes never worn again after the first time.

Dream

Last night I dreamed I was 2000ft in the sky, strapped in an airplane seat

I was counting down the time till I landed at my next destination.

I had inherited a sixth sense of knowing when I was no longer wanted,

and I sure as hell refused to stay.

My grandmother knew a person long, long ago,

he had a crazy dream too.

His was that black and white children could hold hands.

For twenty to thirty years it became true, but now…

it's demolishing right beneath him.

Here

I was never meant to be here.
I had dreams of being faraway,
somewhere I didn't have to force myself to stay,
where my wings could learn to take flight.
Not here.

I was meant to have a soulmate
who makes me forget the inner turmoil
caused by the demons who utterly destroyed me.
We would have been inseparable until death did us apart.
Instead, I lay here alone.

I was supposed to be this world-renowned writer,
my words meant to grab others attention,
to inspire them to reach their own dreams.
My book transformed into movies.

But that will only be a figment of my imagination
because I am here.
I was never meant to be here.

A Mockingbirds Song

The blaring ball of fire became a mockingbird
taking on a persona that was very rarely its own.
Its wingspan opened up, blanketing the newcomers
all robed in fifty shades of black
Transforming them into prey.
Or maybe its song was misheard
when mingled with the underlying grief of the people.
It could have been a song of comfort
sensing the dread and numbness
that seemed to infect the masses.
Feeling emptiness and coldness chatter the bones,
the sun could be trying to bring forth warmth
Or just maybe the sun was no mockingbird at all,
its reflection mirrored its true intentions.
The same could not be spewed of the little black girl
balancing from foot to foot off to the side,
a smile stretched from ear to ear.
Her eyes, however, were as empty as the plot prior till
today.
She felt fake spewing it means a lot to me that you came
when really even she hated that she was here.
She wanted to be left alone
as her mother's new home
completely crafted of wood
Was lowered into the ground.
Becoming one with nature,
she saw in the sun
what was really in herself,
The human mockingbird.

Understanding
For a second, I understood
how deep a knife could reach
as it cuts away more and more
of what protects the inside
the need or fascination
of moving an inch to the right
slicing into the artery
longing to bleed out the hurt

I understood,
how easy it was to reach for scotch or vodka
to have a never-ending supply
just flowing down your throat
until you're near the point of unconsciousness
vomit spilling out of your mouth
your mind clouded to the point
where you can't hold on to one thought
where you don't have to worry
or remember

I understood,
how you could reach for one pill
and end up swallowing twenty
hoping it would only take one more
to make it all go away
because you knew death had to be easier
then wondering if anyone ever noticed
the pain behind your eyes
noticed that it was getting physically harder to breath
that you were drowning

and no one was willing to jump in and save you

~~Empathy~~

Every morning I stare in the mirror
Before I hide my hair behind a scarf
It isn't unruly
But because you ask me to

Every day I work my feet to the bone
Behind the desk in some raggedy shack
Unable to speak a word
Because you told me not to

Every night I come home
to slave by a hot stove
while you sip your expensive bottle
Because that is what women are supposed to do

You took away my identity
my loudness, my hair, and everything between
So, forgive me if I don't cry at your funeral,
empathy is no longer me

The Death of Autumn
She came sweeping in like the autumn winds
embedding herself deep into the soil.
She was the bad seed; but I couldn't see that.
So, I continued to nourish
what couldn't be brought back to life.
I ended up with dirt like the Sahara Desert
with no foreseeable end to the drought.
I thought this could only be a coincidence
as apples and pumpkins pushed through.
But the limbs of the trees became brittle
vulnerable like sculptures made of glass.
The autumns colorful leaves fell away,
Leaving behind lackluster browns and grays

A Letter to Myself
I forgive you, though I don't know what I forgive you for.
I love you, though you have given me nothing to love.
I hear you, though you rarely open your mouth to speak.
I see you, though you try to cloak yourself from me.

Why can't you forgive you, for your inability to sever your pain?
Why can't you love you, without all these worldly restraints?
Why can't you hear you, when you tell yourself you are important?
Why can't you see you, for all that good that you have done?

Hunted

She could feel two sets of eyes boring into her back
Still she didn't move.
She could hear the brittle grass snapping under their paws
Still she sat.
She could smell their hunger for blood get stronger
Yet, she just laid down.
She could taste the victory mere seconds away
She was no longer the hunted.

No More Sorries

He told me he was sorry that he couldn't love me the way I needed,

the same love he turned around and gave to someone else.

She told me she was sorry that she couldn't raise me

as she raised the syringe full of meth.

He told me he was sorry for being absent.

Yet, he willed and prayed for his heart to stop, to be taken from this world.

They told me sorry for my loss as they buried my mother forever,

right beside the emotions I no longer wanted to feel.

The same place I intended to burry these sorries.

Sorries did nothing for me except make me sorrier.

Sorry I chipped away pieces of myself for people I thought would keep them safe.

Pieces I thought I could come back to.

But when I finally did all I found was sorries.

Chronic Attachment Disorder

At three I lost my mother.

She didn't die, she just disappeared.

At seven I was placed in the foster care system.

It was safer than living with a child molester.

At eight I got separated from my siblings.

Apparently, I was a bad seed.

At nine I got placed with my forever family.

I thought all the bad could no longer touch me.

At nine and a half/ ten, I lost one of my biological sisters.

She decided to follow in the footsteps of her uncle.

At seventeen I lost my adoptive mother.

I guess God didn't believe I deserved a mom.

In second grade I banged a classmate's head into a locker.

I thought she was trying to steal my boyfriend.

In fifth grade I made my teacher cry.

I thought it was funny to yell at her and talk shit.

In sixth grade I pushed a teacher.

I was trying to hide the evidence of my wrongdoing.

In seventh grade, I got sent to in school suspension.

I thought it was a great idea to write erotica in math class.

Ninth grade I had uncontrollable bouts of crying.
They were brought on by the smallest of things.
Tenth grade I constantly felt overwhelmed.
I was somewhere I couldn't hope to fit in.
Eleventh grade my concentration started to waiver.
I didn't care if I finished. I just wanted to leave.
Twelfth grade I felt helpless.
I no longer enjoyed anything.

Freshman year of college I began isolating myself.
I didn't want to get attached ever again.
Sophomore year I stared at the lake unseeing.
Praying that someone would be willing to drown me.
Junior year, I had trouble sleeping.
My nightmares consisted of my waking problems.
Senior year, I stared blankly up at the ceiling.
I dug my nails into my skin trying to release everything.

As a kid I was diagnosed with chronic attachment disorder.
I got moved around one too many times.
As an adult I was diagnosed with depression and anxiety.
Because I didn't get treatment for my attachment disorder.

Manifestations for 2020/2021

Ms. Eliza M. Ryder will accomplish these goals.

Accumulate ten thousand plus subscribers on YouTube.

Notice her worth absent of men and absent of friends.

Illustrate how to create an efficient foster care system.

Figure out if she will finish her MSW or apply for MFAs

Enroll back into counseling for depression and anxiety.

Sit with lawyers to iron out legal details of nonprofit.

Take classes to prepare for creating a family.

Accrue money from various revenue to erase school debt.

Turn her many unfinished manuscripts into best sellers.

Identify where she wants to live and purchase a home.

Own a children's shelter and online clothing boutique.

Nurture her talents into their fullest capability.

Set aside time to validate suppressed feelings.

Why I Dream Big

Everyone peers over their drinks at me as if I am crazy when I tell them all the things I will do. I tell them I will be as big as JK Rowling, writing in the styles of Jodi Picoult. They just scoff. My books will be transformed into movies, and my words will change the lives of others. My articles will tell stories of heartaches, heartbreaks, and what it means to be alive. I will own a safe house for abused and neglected children. They look at me with pity and question, "Why do you always gotta dream so big?"

I dream big because my special brother needs a special kind of tutor. His beautiful mind can calculate math facts but struggles to put letters together to make sounds. His art is his body that he rhythmically moves to the beat to tell his story. I dream big for my father, who has had his dreams stolen, and I want him to get them back. He dreams of listening to the sweet lullaby of the ocean while he sits back and fishes. He dreams of being one with the fish underneath the surface, discovering and taking pictures, reaching his true purpose. I dream big for every little child who doesn't deserve to be scared or hurt, who doesn't deserve to be left on their own with no self-defense. I dream big because if I don't, who will?

Wifey Material

They fester over the idea I'm too independent,
jealous I have multiple streams of income coming in.
They assume I slept my way to the top,
I rose too quickly for them to believe I'm efficient.
They want me to settle down, be trapped with a baby.
They're annoyed I won't hand over what is rightfully mine,
and insinuate that I am crazy.
They assume since I love cooking, they can tether me to the kitchen.
Irritated that I don't cater to their every whim, and force them to pitch in.
Yeah, it's true at times I'm the pure definition of wifey.
But I also need to build my empire and leave my children a legacy.

Family

To My Family
I would say they aren't all there
There are a couple of screws loose
They are a basket case
The lights are on, but no one's home
Off their rockers

But I could also say
They are the brightest crayons in the box
Can hit the nail on the head
They are sharp cookies
Walking encyclopedias

I would say they are quick to anger
Party animals
Highly opinionated

But I could also say
They are supportive
Charismatic
Loyal

Questions for Mom
We drew our swords sharpened by love
coated gold in the purest warmth.
Yet, never could we slay the dragon
that hurt you from the inside.

We spent our days in darkness
created by demon's flesh,
and our night in fires
sparked by your hell.

We threw glass bottles
trying to hit a bullseye.
pulling arms back
and letting loose.
We had become the target.

We weren't always like that.

Your godly strength used to catch my luggage
transporting it into your home.
Your nurturing instinct
would wash my hair over the kitchen sink.

Your voice boomed carrying me to home plate,
your encouragement electing me president of NHS.
Your protective instinct conquered the enemy,
that told me I'm not smart enough to belong.
that I could only ever make it so far.

Why couldn't we have gone back to that?

The Five Stages of Grief
When I wake up tomorrow
She won't be dead
she'll still be here.
This is a sick joke everyone is playing on me.
They want to see me break down.
That wasn't her cold body on the bed this morning.
Those aren't real tears.
Everyone must be great actors.
Karma will bite them in the ass for this cruelness.
Why is it happening to me?
I am trying to be a good person dammit.
Maybe if I had stopped arguing with dad all the time
Or got all A's in school she would still be here.
If not, are we allowed to switch places?
You know what, it doesn't matter anymore.
Breathing is stupid.
I know she's gone.
I also accept I'm not okay with it.

Dancing with the Prince
He pulls me in close, he knows I can't dance.
His suggestion. put my feet and hands on top of his.
He twirls me around the dance floor.
He dips me till I'm mere inches from the ground.
My mind has no worries.
I trust him to never drop me.
As the dance comes to an end,
I make sure to cherish every last bit of it.
I can't help the smile that crosses my face.
I got the chance to dance with my dad, the prince.
He's a true knight in shining armor,
who will forever hold a place in my heart,
even after he is no longer here.

Constant Changing
As time remained steady ticking
I forgot about what molded my childhood.
I didn't remember many of the arguments
or the reason for the continuous butt whooping's.
I couldn't remember what mom loved to wear.
Let alone, what she loved to drink.
She always changed it up.
If I couldn't count on anything, I could count on that.
You, however, were my constant,
you and your little white sticks.
I remember you had boxes upon boxes of these white sticks.
Mom would replace them before you could run out.
Even if that meant making that month's budget a little tighter
You'd smoke one before you left for work,
one when you came back,
one while making dinner,
and one before bed.
Even after mom died and everything changed,
I could count on your smoke breaks.
Sure, you begin to smoke in the house
Lord knows you knew how mom hated it.
But it was okay because you were still in a routine.
Imagine my surprise when I came out one day
there was no longer a white cigarette
But a brown cigar.
It was the moment
comfort and dad were no longer in the same sentence.
Routine no longer existed.

I made it my mission to ignore you.
She had finally dug her claws in.
You were no longer my constant,
I refused to let you be.
As time continues to steadily go on
I hope there comes a point in time I won't remember this either.

Biting Words
They say that the pen is mightier than the sword
That fails in comparison to the tongue.
For the pen lays stinging words on the paper
But the tongue is the trigger on the gun
That pierces the soul with a deafening blow
Stunning the lamb just long enough
To be led to the slaughter.

Lost at Sea
For the longest time the sea was your home.
You kept yourself emerged underwater,
because it was the only way you knew to breath.
You chanted over and over in your head
"just keep swimming"
because was the only way you knew how to stay afloat.

But the sea is not where you belong anymore,
You struggle so much just to survive.
Your gills have been plagued with pain,
You learned to live, without being alive.

You used to glide like a baby dolphin
peacefully, through the waves.
Now you've become a vicious shark, poised,
ready to attack the unsuspecting.

As you sink more and more toward the bottom
it makes it hard for any bleeding-heart human
to save you,
for me to save you.

Her Gateway

She snorts cocaine because it's the only way she can get out of bed in the morning,
the only way she can speak up and make sure her voice is heard.
It's the only way she can find any excitement for life.

She drowns herself in alcohol because it's the only way she can mellow out,
the only way she can escape being labeled the angry black woman.
It's the only way she can relate to her emotionally absent father.

She pops pain killers because it's the only she can dream of a better tomorrow,
the only way she can stop being haunted by nightmares playing on a loop.
It's the only way she can feel anything other than numbness.

She takes LSD because it's the only way she can have a relationship with God, the only way she can let go off all the resentment she has towards him.

It's the only way she cannot blame him for the death of her mother.

She has multiple sexual partners because it is the only way she feels desirable,

the only way she can afford the nicer things in life.

It's the only way she can feel deserving of love.

To My Biological Mother,

Sometimes when I think of all the times you've hurt me and mistreated my trust; I can't help but wonder if I will ever be able to forgive you. I watched you go in and out of rehab until I was taken away by the state. Every kid in my classroom had a mother but me. You continuously chose the drugs. You left us in the hands of a demented person. You knew he had sexually assaulted one of your children, and still, you did nothing. Not then, and definitely not now. Every now and again, when I visit, you mention how much you love him and how you need to go visit your precious brother. Do you even care how many lives he destroyed? That same child he assaulted, turned around, and assaulted someone else, and the vicious cycle didn't stop with them. What if I became one of his victims? I was three when you left me with him. How does a three-year-old defend themselves? I refuse to be dragged into that horror and that cycle. I am terrified to have kids because I don't want them to end up like any of you.

You finally got clean when I no longer needed you. Since then, you love to play the victim. "You were only on drugs because someone you love and trusted gave them to you." Truth is, you didn't have to take them. That was your decision. I get how addiction works, but you forget an addiction doesn't form unless you've ingested the substance. You lash out at my adoptive mother, and you claim that she turned us against you, but you don't realize, she was there when you weren't. She made sure I had food to eat, clothes on my back, a shelter over my head. She cheered me on at softball games, drove me to and from cheer practice, and helped me get lessons when I wanted to join the competition choir. She took the time to know me and make sure I grew into a reputable young woman. She set me up for my best chance. You couldn't even take your classes or complete counseling in a timely manner for us. You had a chance to still be in contact via open adoption. Selfishly, you chose not to, all because you didn't want to share us, and you were worried about what your fucked-up family might think.

 I still remember the time when we were in foster care, and we were asked in front of you if we wanted to go back with you or be adopted. You promised you wouldn't get mad no matter the answer. I told you I wanted to stay where I was. You got so angry. You complained that I hated you, and you tried to turn my siblings against me. You told them that I didn't love you. It's funny because back then, I thought I did. I foolishly believed that every child must love their mother, but now I realize, how can you love someone you don't know?

The Gap

The first gap came in the form of a needle as you injected yourself with your life saving substance. The one you said relieved you of the mental pain that continued to drag you under, drowning you.

The second gap came in the form of you placing me in a figurative box on the doorstep of your demented brother. You filled that gap with a plea to me to forgive you, that you're only trying to get better.

The third gap came in the form of you never returning till it was too late. The needle and plea stayed present wedged between us, leaving no room for me in your life. So, I left in hopes that these things between us would no longer be trapped, having somewhere to go.

The first time you tried bridging the gap began with your voice drifting in and out of my telephone. It found me standing over a body of water on a pier wondering what would happen if I just sunk down to the bottom.

You never tried again, and I became forever grateful for the space that you forged between mother and daughter.

To My Little Girl

The evening I left I thought you would still be there when I came back.
Still in your worn kneed khakis and clean pressed shirt.
Your hair would still be neatly braided and shoulder length
And you smile forever carved on your face.
But that wasn't fair of me to ask, was it?

I couldn't deny you the same happiness that was once gifted to me.
The chance to feel sunlight washing through your hair
To feel the grass tickling the bottoms of your tiny feet.
I couldn't be the one to steal your voice,
To take away your song.
I couldn't be the one to step on your feet as you danced your story.
That would be selfish of me, wouldn't it?

So, I forced myself to be happy that you moved on
From this place and from me.
But as time went on, I adjusted to your absence.
I no longer had to force myself.
I was truly happy for you.
I began to try and make other attachments.

Then one day you appeared back in front of me,

Throwing your arms around me in a warm greeting.

There was that smile and that braided hair.

I wanted to start bawling, knowing you were back here.

Life became ironic, didn't it?

Backdoor

They all study the peculiar human who never uses the front door.

For her, it always has to be the back.

It's there where she finds the most room to grow

and there where she finds forgiveness.

She never chooses the answer agreed upon by everyone else

She always chooses her own.

For it's there she gains the most knowledge and

there she learns how to live with her mistakes.

She never gives time to the world; it never had the time to stop for her.

For it's the only way she knows she'll arrive at her destination

and the only way she knows no one will get in her way.

Faceless Creature
The faceless creature came knocking at the door,
Some of his features I thought I saw before.
Eyes brown as tree bark, skin the color of Hershey bars
His temple on the right side held a crescent shaped scar.
I remembered him smelling of stale cigarettes,
with tiny hints of sweat.
When he came, he didn't come alone.
Standing behind him was a woman made of bones.
She was the perfect blonde featured in books,
Her face permanently etched with this unforgiving look.
It screamed, "Why am I here? I am better than you,"
Considering the circumstances, I guess that was true.
Eventually I learned why that face looked so familiar,
that was a face I saw every time I look in the mirror.
As introduction were made my eyes began to water,
I learned that familiar but faceless creature was my father.

To My Biological Father,

It's crazy how everyone thinks I look just like you. When I was younger, I used to stare at myself in the mirror and wonder what you were like. Did you spend hours staring at yourself in the mirror wondering about me? Even if you did, it doesn't matter now. It hurts how I can count on one hand the times I saw you as a child. And those four or five times weren't all pleasant. I remember the year you showed up on Christmas with the white woman and her children or the time we went to visit you at your mothers and learned they were living with you. It was impossible for me to comprehend how you could take care of someone else's kids but refused to take care of your own. You could live with someone else's kids but refuse to visit yours more than twice a year.

Now that I'm twenty-four, you love to remind me that you are here now and how your feelings get hurt when I mention my adoptive father. But that's not fair. You came back into my life after I was already an adult. It made me feel like you only wanted to be there now because you no longer had to take responsibility for me. You claim that you want to get to know me, your daughter. How can you get to know me without getting to know the man who raised me? He brought me an ice cream cone the first time that we met, when they were looking into what placement would be best. It wasn't much, but it at least showed me that he cared and was willing to be present even though we were not his own. He continued to be present for many years after. He showed up to my softball, basketball, and volleyball games. He showed up to every single concert I had in high school. He was there to watch me walk across the stage for both eighth grade and high school. He was the one cheer dad at competition who learned how to straighten hair and do makeup because he didn't want me to stick out like a sore thumb from the other girls. He taught me how to shoot for my dreams and to never give up in the face of adversity. This strong, resilient, beautiful, and independent woman you see standing right in front of you, he made. So, you see there would be no me without him and I should be allowed to speak about him when I please. You, you shouldn't be jealous or curse the very ground he walks on. He did what you couldn't do.

Friends

Friends?

I wish I could say once you hit a certain age you become okay with the idea of being alone,
of being no one's person.

That you come to terms with the fact that your face will always be the one attached to the camera trying to remember these moments. knowing no one cares to remember you're there.

I wish I could promise that you would be able to speak your mind without the fear of others speaking over you or not paying attention.

I wish I could tell you they'll be there at your lowest moments just like you were during theirs, that they would support your dreams when they seem ludicrous.

But I can't. All I can do is tell you, no ask you, to never change. Friends will come and go just as the storms do, but you must not let that dictate who you become.

To My High School Best Friend

I'd rather not have loved, then to have loved and lost

Cuts

She smiles whenever we are together.
She laughs over the telephone.
She walks with flowers on her head.
Sings the words to every musical.
She is always loyal to me.
She trusts in me no matter what.
We hang out everyday sipping Starbucks,
Which makes it harder that I didn't know.

She doesn't see the beauty I see.
She only sees a glob.
I think she wants to eat healthy.
She doesn't want to eat at all.
Her smile hides pain.
Her laugh covers fear
When I thought she was just dancing in the rain,
She was really looking for a way to hide her tears.
I call myself her best friend
but I didn't know this.
How could I have not known
she cuts?

Support System

You are the smile that breaks through the storm clouds

The hands that glue me together as I fall apart

The feet that move me forward,

The stomach that fills me with unconditional love

Together you have become my heart of steel, unbreakable.

Best Friend

My heart breaks writing this
Yet, I am joyful all the same.

My sophomore year we met,
And by senior year we were inseparable.
Galloping to New Orleans chasing your dream,
In Indianapolis you left me.
Can you please come home to me?

Unfortunately, this is not where you belong
Nor is it where you want to stay.
I know New York is the end goal
Cause you need to make it big.
Oscars will be thrown at you, you'll be
Ranked at the top of your game
No matter how much it hurts, I'll still be cheering you on.

Snapshot

I tell you it's a bad idea
You decide to do it anyway
I end up face palming hard
As you admit I'm right like always

I'm the only one you trust with him
Love Bug is my second son
You both like to chill in my room
and talk about the dates we've been on

We question Spencer's salt intake
Squeal about Americas ass
We almost die trying to wash Cammy
And serve our bosses tons of sass.

These are just some of my favorite snapshots
Of when we used to live on Parkway
Spencer and Heather if you are reading this
The dishes need cleaning and it's your day.

Fireball

After God created Fireball he stopped.

He knew he'd made his greatest creation yet

He sprinkled in just the right amount of cinnamon

To counteract a great fiery kick.

When consumed by others it goes down smooth.

He slapped a red dragon on the front

to demonstrate its passion and generosity.

He named it fireball to warn others who abused it

They will get burned.

The Traveler

The traveler slips away in the dark of the night.

Leaving behind no evidence of where's she's going,

Only where she's been.

The traveler destroys all romantic relationships

She believes it's best to have no connections.

She doesn't want to be held back.

The traveler is worried she'll never learn to love.

She already has.

By sharing stories of where she's been

She gives tiny glimpses of where she's going.

Showing that she has hopes and dreams for tomorrow

Hopes and dreams that only true friends would understand.

Though the traveler slips away in the darkness

With us, she'll never truly be alone.

T.H.O.T is My Friend

That man over there is one big ball of crazy.
He is also talented beyond belief.
Only one who can say some of the shit he does
Then turn around and not receive any grief.
I think he was dropped on his head as a baby and I
Swear he sniffed one too many sharpies.
My guess is that's how they do it over in Cali.
Yet if it's only him, wouldn't surprise me.
Fine, I'm done joking about this man
Really, I won't mention his hoeish ways,
Instead I'll talk about why we're his biggest fans.
Ehhh… my mind has drawn a blank, no nice words to say
Naw, bro I'm just playing. Let me get for real.
Dude, I swear, one day I'll communicate how I truly feel.

Just Dance Slayer
Oh, how she makes me drink water
And tucks my drunk self in at night
You don't know how much I love her
And her iridescent light

She makes sure I don't dance on strangers
Grabs me when I run from the cops
She's quick to defend all the waiters
From immature boys who won't stop

She twerks like Tina, her idol
And kicks butt at Just Dance
She has the name mom as a title
You can see it with one glance

For the Boys
If you tell her the weekends are for the boys
She'll just join in anyway
She fits in with the best of them
On any given day

If you tell her she can join in
She'll take it one step further
She will beat you at your own game
While being a head turner

If you tell her she looks amazing
She'll say she got it from her momma
and if you ain't her favorite frat boy
she ain't here for all the drama

If you're here to bring her drama sweetie
You might as well just stay at home
She'll destroy your entire weekend
Then leave you on your own

LOVE

Validation

I.

My love came in the form of expensive chocolates I took great care of placing in your locker. The mint chocolate once a reminder of fresh starts became a symbolization of the way you iced me out. The gradually melting dark chocolate was a reminder of how you leisurely churned me into the perfect bitter batter. While the peanut chocolate became an agitation that forced a distancing reaction that wasn't present before, forever scarring me away from love in fear of anaphylactic shock.

II.

My love for chocolate dissipated leaving my stomach gurgling and my heart with an emptiness begging to be filled again. I went searching in the fields adjacent to my house trying to fill this hole with nature. I stumbled across chirping birds sunbathing unaware of the dangers lurking just outside their ecosystem. There you were, a beautiful soft pink flower, enticing me and painting me as if I was a bee- your only chance of survival. Foolishly, I allowed myself to believe this as true drinking in your nectar like a starved man quenching his thirst. I never once questioned if you were poisonous or if the relationship was toxic and doomed.

III.

Your cancerous toxins transformed a loyal bitch into a snake. There were days I pawed at the front door enthusiastically waiting your arrival. Now I just slither between the cracks left in my armor trying to escape. Nights where I nestled into your side whimpering for an ounce of love turned into wistfully wishing my body would constrict around your neck. Knowing death was too kind of a punishment, I instead slithered away leaving you to your own devices.

IV.

Slithering away to my next destination I shed the skin of a lovesick fool to make room for the commitment-phobe seductress you turned me into. My body hypnotizing the unfortunate souls unlucky enough to stumble within the two walls of my garden. Enthralled by the one lone flower with drooping petals unable to support its own weight. Nourishment from the chocolate soil had become blocked off by an invisible and impenetrable barricade resurrected as a defense mechanism.

Man Enough

I never once said that to be a true man you were required to rake in the dough.
Nor did I say you were required to pay for my meal all the times we went out.
I never once asked you to run up the mileage on your mother's new black BMV.
Nor did I ask you to show up on my doorstep every time you were in town.
You did all that on your own

I never once asked for you to lavish me with gifts on my birthday,
or empty out your bank account on Christmas.
I never once asked you to apologize for focusing on your mental health
or to have your entire life figured out.
You did all that on your own.

You did it because you thought that was what made you man enough.

All I asked was for you to communicate in a reasonable time frame
and to not leave me on read when I share what's troubling me.
to not cause a scene every time I paid for my own things and
keep the promises/ plans you made with me.
That would have made you man enough for me.

But you couldn't do that.

Fix You

Your eyes sit at half mass
Pills sit on your bedside table untouched.
The kitchen hasn't felt your presence in days
and your hair hasn't been done in months.

Your bed is your new lover
The pillow has become your support.
Your parents can no longer get through to you
ignoring others has become your favorite sport.

You no longer feel any type of emotion
Body language as frigid as the winters cold.
The ability to pick up a phone has disappeared
Seeing a therapist has gotten old.

Across the city I sit dumbfounded
Still unsure of what to do.
I had to learn to put myself first
and understand I couldn't fix you.

If You Have Mercy

We lay back to back in the same bed we used to lay chest to chest. You used to lift my head up off the pillow only to replace it with your body. Now those same limbs keep me at arm's length. When I finally worked up the nerve to question the distance, you whispered into the dark that nothing has changed. Nothing may have changed for you, but everything has changed for me.

Somewhere along the road I stopped being content with watching you sneak out long before the sun had a chance to arise and the little kisses I received only when no one was looking. You became discontent with the girl who actually followed the rules of our arrangement and who learned how to speak up for herself when she learned out you weren't.

And though you became so discontent with her you refused to let her go, playing a mind game that she never had a chance of winning. You constantly took as she constantly gave, refusing to take turns. Just when she decided she finally had enough, you would give the smallest inch. As she tried to walk away, you would put up obstacles in the form of words you thought she wanted to hear, tricking her into believing she owed you.

"I've only ever been with you."
"You are so beautiful and amazing."

And just when she fell for it hook, line, and sinker you made sure to switch up, to let her know exactly what you thought of her.

"This was never more than anything but fun."
"The only reason you are leaving is because you want to bust it open for someone else."

What was there for her to say? No amount of words could change the opinion he had somehow constructed in his delusional brain and she was tired of the jabs at her self-esteem. All she could do was pack up the hopes and dreams she had once held for them and pen out her final goodbye.

"If you have even an ounce of love for me, just have mercy."
"Let me move on. Let me find happiness away from you"

Cater

I want to be catered to.
I want doors opened and chairs pulled out
to be shown off while we are out and about.
I want to come home to a home cooked meal,
for you to take into consideration how I feel.
I want a bath to be drawn as I finish up for the night,
for once I want to say I'm wrong and you were right.
I want to be catered to,
the same way I cater to you.

A Woman Scorned
You fear no evil as your eyes drink in my beauty
Your calloused hands embrace the pearl white
Sometimes lilac, baby bottomed smooth skin.
My dome droops over protecting my precious pistol inside
The antidote for all healthy men
Comes in the form of my fire red berries.

You fear no evil as the wool draws over your eyes
And the heart that beats every second reduces to every fourth.
Your marvelous skin becomes painted with blotches of red
And the ropes of your digestive system get tied
in boy scout knots drawn tight to the point of searing pain.

Though you walk through the valley of death
Made from the illusions of my enthralling beauty
You still choose to fear no evil.

Safe

Maybe if we hide underground
Or make a nest up in the trees
Maybe if we close our eyes and make no sound
They won't come for you or me.

Maybe if we set sail upon the seas
Or take a plane to some deserted land
Maybe if I beg and plead on my knees
They would have some mercy and understand.

But these are just ignored wishes
Made on burnt out fallen stars
A once beautiful dream turned vicious
Tainted by those looking to sketch scars.

Troubles caused by two people fighting over who's is bigger
Two dumbasses in a relationship with our hands posed on the trigger.

Laws and Attraction

Ordained

Yet disparaged

Quiet seduction lures

What lurking forces part

Star-crossed

Cover Me

My body folds into your frozen silhouette

only moving when you do.

My eyes train on the heartbeat

pulsing sporadically under my hand.

I listen for the tears that sit in bowls

continuously feeling up, but never overflowing.

My mouth gulps down the hurt that rolls

off your form in waves.

To My Nature Boy

Your hair is the sun as it begins to set in the evening sky,
golden yellow and orange strands I continuously weave through my fingers.

Your eyes are the ocean,
aquamarine blue, clear, and no ending in sight.

Your body is the tree in my backyard with millions of tiny white petals,
a shelter from life's storms.

Your lips are the strawberries nestled between the creamer and chocolate,
red and very sweet to the taste.

Your laugh is the sound of the American robins sitting outside my window,
melodious, loud, and constant.

You my little nature boy are my everything.

My Quiet Strength

Oh, how you stand majestically in front of the crowd looking down.
Your red six-inch stilettos clicking to their own beat
I stand enraptured as your hands whiz back and forth
As if they are telling the story.
I am even more in love with this persona of you,
a stark contrast from our moments alone.

I would sit on the couch pretending to read,
Yet my eyes never steering far from you for too long.
I'd watch enchanted as your pearly white teeth gnawed
At your blush pink lips and
your hands push your hint of orange hair behind your ear.
I'm soothed by the strokes of your ivory fingers on the keyboard.
Reminding me that your looks aren't the only thing I love about you.

I am stunned by your ability to take control when I self-doubt
The way your intelligence shines through your words.
I am enamored by the soft giggles you share with everybody else

And voluminous snorts you share only with me.

I am dazzled by the way you are never over the top
But also, never make yourself small for others.
My quiet strength, you are my everything.

St. Louis

I left my heart in Saint Louis knowing there was no way I'd get it back.

I left knowing I would never again see its long dreads or two miniature tattoos resting at the crease of its eyes.

I would never feel the touch of its gentle hands caressing the skin on my back where my shirt fell loosely off my shoulder.

I left knowing I would never taste its lips that gently spoke truth into my soul.

I left my heart in St. Louis knowing I'll never get it back because sometimes love just isn't enough.

What Was Best

Your grandmother told me about you four months before we actually met. How you were an intelligent young man who was striving for his masters. She failed to mention, you could make anyone fall under your spell. Our friendship began in a Wednesday night class over a borrowed laptop and smile. And continued to grow as we grew.

We bonded over the idea that we have to let our siblings learn from their own mistakes since they refused to learn from ours. You whispered into my ear secrets that I have kept to this day. Our "dates" consisted of walks to the vending machines and splitting a box of Save-a-Lot animal crackers. The professors found it crazy that our seats never found their way very far from each other and some part of our bodies were always touching. Everything about us was great until I received the call about my father in the hospital fighting for his life. That was the first time I walked away. The second came in the form of me sneaking out once your grandfather's funeral ended. I toyed with the idea of finding you and consoling you. I watched as you crumpled in on yourself unable to hold yourself up anymore. I wished I could have peered into your eyes hidden behind black glasses. But I couldn't do that to you. I was and forever will be toxic, a girl who never learned to love.

When I came back three months later, I can't promise that I hadn't already made up my mind about leaving again, but for good this time. No matter how loved you made me feel I couldn't get over this deep-rooted feeling that I was suffocating. As I told you this, I thought you would hate me, but all you did was wrap me up in a hug that lasted half a minute at most but felt like hours. You told me to do what was best for me and that no matter where I go to make sure I finished what I started. Your parting words stay seared in my brain, "I can't believe I'm losing you again. I just got you back."

Though I know I would never be happy in Saint Louis, I can't help but wonder what would have happened if I never left? Or if I went back? Would it be worth it coming up to visit you? But I let my questions be just that. I don't allow myself to want the answers, cause either way one of us will end up hurting. I showed you love in the only way I knew how. by letting whatever we had be washed away in the tide, letting you go. I couldn't be selfish. I had to allow you the chance to have someone love you the same way you loved me.

With Silence
I try to go after you, but my feet won't move.
I try to scream to you, but my voice is broken.
I want to reach out to you, but my hands just tremble at my side.
I want to say I love you, but I can't find the words.
I know I am crying but I can't feel or taste the salty tears.
So, I let you go and wish for you to be happy,
with silence

My Vows to You

I promise to love me above all else, to continuously put me first. I promise to fill up my own cup before I try to pull into others, to make sure all holes are patched.

I promise to never stop reaching for the stars, to keep grinding until I'm positive my children and grandchildren will be covered long after I'm gone. I promise to validate your pain as much as I validate others, to give you the space to meditate and heal.

All of my friends, I promise to love you even in the moments you refuse to love yourself, to pick you up whenever you fall. I promise to always be present to celebrate your greatest achievements, to coax you through your trials. I promise to continue oversharing fantasies and experiences, to listen when you do the same. I promise to always be truthful even in the moments when it hurts, to always pour into you.

Every day from here till my deathbed, my kin, I promise to do everything in my power to make sure each and every one of you are taken care of emotionally, physically, mentally, and some day economically, to help with school and work assignments. I promise to talk you down when you are close to the edge, to ensure your bodies and minds are fed. I promise to continue showing up to graduations, birthday parties and the births of my nieces and nephews, to remind you that your dreams are worth reaching for. I promise to show you that you are more than your parent's sin, to show you that it's not on you to take the blame. I promise to always talk shit about you, to beat anyone who tries to do the same. I promise to always pour into you.

Until it's time for God to call me home, the love of my life, I promise to cherish you, to spoil you. I promise to always root for you, to be a shoulder to cry on. I promise to never belittle you or absent mindedly write off your wants and needs, to never intentionally hurt you. I promise to continuously build with you, to create a legacy. I promise to be your best friend, to be your lover. I promise to cook, if you do the dishes, to do the laundry if you are willing to fold and put it away. I promise to put no one before you except God, to pour into you.

www.ingramcontent.com/pod-product-compliance
Lightning Source LLC
Chambersburg PA
CBHW030812090426
42736CB00028B/1319